A CANDLE FOR GRANDPA

A Guide to the Jewish Funeral
for Children and Parents

◆ ◆ ◆

DAVID TECHNER and
JUDITH HIRT-MANHEIMER

Illustrated by JOEL ISKOWITZ

UAHC PRESS · NEW YORK, NEW YORK

This book is dedicated with gratitude
to all of my teachers;
the kids of the Detroit Jewish community,
whose openness, honesty, and curiosity
have been an inspiration to me;
and to their parents,
who placed their trust in me.

Also, to Ari, Chad, and Stephanie,
who have made being a father
my greatest gift.

To Ilene, whose love, support, and encouragement
have made this book a reality.

And to Alicia, of blessed memory.
You are forever in our thoughts.
—*David Techner*

For Diana Hirt, of blessed memory.
—*Judith Hirt-Manheimer*

Preface

Until the twentieth century, most people died at home, not in hospitals or nursing homes. Children were not shielded from death, which was accepted as natural. Today, children often learn about death from watching violent scenes on television and in films. As a result, many children think that all deaths are frightful and bloody. A funeral provides children with an opportunity to confront their concerns, to have their questions answered, and to join family members in celebrating the life of the person who has died.

In the pages that follow, we present a story that introduces young children to a traditional Jewish funeral. It should be noted, however, that Jewish burial practices vary significantly from community to community.

The story is followed by responses to the five most common questions that children and parents ask before a funeral and by a glossary.

We wish to acknowledge with gratitude the indispensable assistance of Stuart Benick, Dr. Jane Evans, Rabbi Earl Grollman, Hannah Hirt, Dr. Norman Hirt, Aron Hirt-Manheimer, Herb Kaufman, Rabbi Robert Orkand, Kathy Parnass, Dr. Berit Reisel, Rabbi M. Robert Syme, Rabbi Bernard Zlotowitz, and the staff of the Ira Kaufman Chapel.

We are lighting a *yahrzeit* candle in memory of Grandpa Morris. He died one year ago on this day. I was ten at the time. My sister Becky was seven, and my other sister, Nicole, was four.

I remember that we were eating dinner in the kitchen. The phone rang, and Mom picked it up. It was Grandma Sarah. I could tell from the look on Mom's face that something was wrong. She told Grandma, "I'll meet you at the hospital."

Mom said that her father, Grandpa Morris, had a heart attack and that an ambulance was taking him to the hospital. Becky wanted to see the ambulance. Mom said that it would be better if she stayed home. Mom promised to phone us as soon as she knew how Grandpa Morris was. Nicole grabbed Mom's legs. She didn't want her to go. I just went to my room.

A few hours later, Mom called. From my room, I heard Dad say, "I'll tell the children." Dad asked Becky and me to sit close to him on the living room sofa. Nicole was already asleep. Dad said in a low voice, "I have something very sad to tell you. Grandpa Morris just died." We were quiet for a few minutes. Then Dad said, "He was a wonderful man who loved you very much."

Dad looked so sad. It was the first time I can remember seeing tears in his eyes. Becky asked if the doctors could fix Grandpa's heart and make him live again. Dad explained that a person who dies cannot be brought back to life, even by the best doctors. I couldn't believe that Grandpa was dead. I didn't want to believe it.

Dad told us that Mom was going to be very busy helping Grandma Sarah arrange the funeral. Becky wanted to know what people do at a funeral. Dad explained that it was a special service held for a person who died. Friends and family get together at the funeral to say good-bye and remember that person.

Becky asked if children go to funerals. Dad answered that he didn't know. Becky said she wanted to say good-bye to Grandpa. Dad promised to discuss the matter with Mom. Becky asked me if I wanted to go to the funeral. I told Becky to stop asking so many questions. "What's the matter?" she shouted. "Don't you care about Grandpa?" I wanted to hit her.

Dad asked Becky to bring the family photo album

from the bookshelf. We sat for a long time looking at pictures of Grandpa Morris. In the pictures, he was happy and having fun with us. In one picture, he and I were about to play catch with the new baseball mitt that I had asked him to get me for my sixth birthday. In another picture, Grandpa was helping Becky ride her bike without training wheels. On the next page, there was a picture of Grandpa Morris and Grandma Sarah in the synagogue at the baby-naming ceremony for Nicole. Looking at the pictures felt strange. But remembering all our good times with Grandpa Morris made us smile.

That night, I couldn't fall asleep. My mind was filled with questions. Why couldn't I cry? Why didn't I want to go to the funeral? Did Becky think that I had no feelings for Grandpa Morris? I didn't understand what was going on.

In the morning, Mom hugged all of us for a long time. At breakfast, she told us that Grandma Sarah would be staying with us for the *shivah* period, the seven days after a funeral when family and friends gather to remember the person who has died. Dad explained that we need to comfort one another at sad times. Becky said that was why she wanted to go to the funeral. Mom replied that she understood and then told us a story.

When Mom was six, her grandmother died. Mom wanted to go to the funeral, but her parents decided that she should stay home with a baby-sitter. Mom was very sad. She felt as though her grandmother had just disappeared. Mom missed saying good-bye to her grandma. That's why she thought it might be a good idea for us to go to the funeral. "But before Dad and I decide what to do," she said, "I want us all to meet with the funeral director. We have an appointment with Mr. Rosen after breakfast. He will explain what will happen at the funeral."

Mr. Rosen met us at the entrance of the funeral home and took us into his office. He gave us juice and cookies and said he would answer our questions. Becky asked, "Where is Grandpa Morris?" Nicole wanted to know if she could save some cookies for Grandpa. Mom and Dad looked uncomfortable. Mr. Rosen said that these were good questions and promised to answer them before we left.

Mr. Rosen explained that when someone close to us dies and we feel sad, our Jewish tradition helps us during this difficult time. It teaches us what prayers to say and how to care for the dead person's body.

Mr. Rosen wanted us to know that Grandpa Morris's body was never left alone. A person called a *shomer*, which means "guard," stayed with him and said special prayers. The people who prepare a body for burial belong to a group called the *Chevrah Kadisha*. "Serving as a member of this group brings great honor," said Mr. Rosen, "because a dead person cannot give thanks or reward you. Nor does a member of the *Chevrah Kadisha* expect anything in return."

Before the funeral, the *Chevrah Kadisha* will wash and dress Grandpa Morris in a service called *taharah*, which means "purifying" or "cleaning." Mr. Rosen compared *taharah* to the washing of a newborn baby who is beginning life in this world. According to Jewish tradition, a person who has died is washed before he or she begins a new life—the time when that person's soul joins God. As they wash Grandpa Morris, the members of the *Chevrah Kadisha* will say prayers.

Dad told Mr. Rosen that Grandpa was brought up in an Orthodox home and would have wanted a traditional funeral. Mr. Rosen said that is why the *Chevrah Kadisha* will dress Grandpa in a shroud after the *taharah* service.

This simple white gown,
he explained, shows that
everyone, rich or poor,
is created equal before God.

The funeral director told us that before Grandpa Morris's body is put into a long wooden box called a casket or coffin, the *Chevrah Kadisha* will include a little bag of soil from Israel. That way, Grandpa Morris's body will always be touching earth from the land of the Jewish people, even though he is being buried in a nearby cemetery.

Next, Mr. Rosen showed us the funeral chapel, the place where the service was going to be held. It looked a little like a synagogue. Our rabbi would lead the service. Mr. Rosen said that Rabbi Levy planned to speak with everyone in our family before the funeral to learn more about Grandpa Morris. Rabbi Levy will tell everyone at the funeral the story of Grandpa Morris's life in a speech called a eulogy.

Mr. Rosen also showed us the place where Grandpa Morris's casket would be from the time we arrive at the funeral home until the time we leave for the cemetery. Becky asked if we could see Grandpa Morris. Mom and Dad answered that we would not see Grandpa Morris but that we could attend the funeral if we wanted.

Mr. Rosen explained that what children imagine about death is much worse than what they see at a funeral. On television and in movies, the bodies of dead people are often battered and bloody. Grandpa Morris looks almost the way he always did, but he is no longer alive. When he died, his body stopped working. Every part of his body is still there, but none of it works. He has eyes but can't see, legs but can't walk, a mouth but can't speak. He has no need to eat or drink or go to the bathroom. That's why we don't have to save any cookies for him.

Mr. Rosen then led us into a garage, where two big cars were parked. He said that the one called a hearse would take the casket to the cemetery. The other car, a limousine, would follow the hearse. Becky asked Mr. Rosen if the limo had a television. "Just seats," he replied. "The large limo makes it possible for close relatives to go to the funeral and cemetery together."

From the garage, Mr. Rosen led us to a big metal room. He said it was a giant refrigerator that kept Grandpa Morris's body very cold. Becky asked what would happen to a dead body that is not kept cold. Mr. Rosen said that the skin would turn black and blue because blood is no longer flowing through the body. He asked Becky what would happen if a friend punched her hard in the arm. "I would punch her back," Becky said. We all laughed. Then Mr. Rosen said, "I mean, what would happen to your arm?" Becky replied that she would get a black and blue mark. "Exactly," said Mr. Rosen, "and that is because no blood would be flowing through that spot. By keeping a body very cold, we make sure that its color will not change."

I asked why dead people are buried in a cemetery. Mr. Rosen replied that after a person's body stops working, it must be put somewhere. He explained that a cemetery is a special place where people can go to visit the graves of family members and friends who have died.

We then went to a room that was filled with different kinds of caskets. Mr. Rosen showed us the casket in which Grandpa Morris's body was going to be buried. "A simple wood casket, like a shroud, shows us that we are all created equal before God," said Mr. Rosen. He opened the empty casket so we could look inside.

When we got home, I felt less nervous. Thanks to Mr. Rosen, I knew what to expect. Thanks to the Jewish tradition, I would be able to say good-bye to Grandpa Morris the same way that he had said good-bye to his grandparents and parents after they died. I was ready to share my sadness with other people who also loved Grandpa Morris.

We drove back to the funeral home. Many of our relatives and friends had already arrived. Being together made us all feel very close. Rabbi Levy pinned a black ribbon to Grandma Sarah's and Mom's dresses. Then the *keriah* prayer was said and the ribbons were cut. The rabbi explained that tearing clothes or cutting a ribbon shows that death has separated us from Grandpa Morris. We say the *keriah* prayer "Blessed are you, O Ruler of the universe, Judge of truth" to declare that even at times of great sadness, our faith in God remains strong.

At the beginning of the service, the rabbi read a poem called a psalm. In his eulogy, Rabbi Levy said that Grandpa cared very much about other people and was always ready to help anyone in need. The rabbi also said that Grandpa Morris enjoyed being with his grandchildren more than he enjoyed anything else. At that moment, I felt very proud.

After the eulogy, the rabbi said more prayers. Then the cantor chanted the *El Malei Rachamim*, asking God to protect Grandpa Morris's soul. When the service ended, my four uncles and two family friends went up to Grandpa Morris's closed casket and carried it out to the waiting hearse. We joined Grandma Sarah in the limousine. Our relatives and friends got into their cars and lined up behind us with their headlights on. Then the hearse led the long line of cars to the cemetery. Nicole fell asleep on the way.

From a distance, the cemetery looked like a park filled with grass and trees. As we got closer, I could see rows of gravestones. When we reached the place where Grandpa Morris was to be buried, we all got out. The six men carried the casket from the hearse and put it on a platform over a deep hole in the ground, next to a pile of dirt.

We gathered around, and Rabbi Levy recited a prayer. Then the casket was lowered slowly into the grave, and the rabbi shoveled some dirt into the hole. Other people, including Becky and me, did the same. Soon the casket was covered. Then the cantor chanted the *El Malei Rachamim* again. The rabbi said more prayers, and family members recited a special *Kaddish*.

I could hear Grandma Sarah crying. I whispered, "Good-bye, Grandpa Morris, I love you." My throat felt as if I had swallowed a baseball. I knew at that moment that Grandpa Morris was never coming back. Becky blew a kiss toward the grave. I took her hand, and we walked away together. Grandpa Morris would have liked that.

One year has passed since Grandpa Morris died. I think about him often. I missed him at my birthday party this year and during the Jewish holidays. I think of him now as I watch the *yahrzeit* candle burn, and I know that the good times we had together will always be a part of me.

I love you, Grandpa Morris.

The Five Questions
Parents Most Frequently Ask

1. Should a child be allowed to attend a funeral?

The key consideration is a child's relationship to the person who died. For example, if the mother of a very young child has died, the best response to the inevitable stream of questions the child will ask about the loss that has so suddenly changed his or her life might be to allow the child to attend the funeral. An important factor in making this decision is evaluating the child's ability to participate without disrupting the proceedings. If a child still wants to attend the funeral after being told what happens there, parents should acknowledge that desire, although the decision is ultimately theirs.

2. Should my child be permitted to view the body?

If a child wants to see the body, several factors must be considered. First, keep in mind what the child would see if he or she is allowed to view the body. If the person died after a long illness and the child had witnessed physical changes in the person, the child's viewing of the body might not be too frightening. However, if the person's death is sudden, the child's viewing of the body might be very upsetting, although his or her confrontation with the physical reality of death might still be advisable. If the child is going to see the body, you can prepare her or him by talking about what he or she can expect to see. Remember that a child often has the same need as an adult to say good-bye to a loved one. (Note that at traditional Jewish funerals, the body is not viewed. However, identification of the body by immediate family members may take place any time prior to the chapel service.)

3. If a child attends the funeral, should he or she also go to the cemetery?

Often a child will find the chapel service more emotionally draining than the brief graveside service. If a child attends the chapel service and then is told that he or she is going home instead of to the cemetery, the child is likely to ask, "Where are you going?" and "Why can't I come, too?" Nothing that happens at the cemetery is beyond a child's comprehension, if it is properly explained beforehand. What the child who is sent home might imagine is generally worse than what he or she would have seen.

4. One of my children seems totally unaffected by a death in the family. My other child is having great difficulty adjusting. Do I need to do anything in response?

Extreme situations can produce extreme and often unpredictable reactions. Therefore, making sure that your children know you are there for them at such times is essential. One way of helping your children express themselves is to set aside time for them to discuss their feelings about death with you. The amount of time you allocate is not as important as your setting aside a designated time in which your children can express their perceptions and feelings. Be prepared for some very tender and meaningful discussions. As a result, you and your children will establish an open line of communication that can have a positive effect on all aspects of your relationship.

5. Since the recent death of a family member, my children have found occasions such as birthdays, anniversaries, and holidays particularly painful. What can I do to help them at such times?

People often find the first birthday, anniversary, or major holiday after a loved one's death the most difficult because such occasions accentuate the sense of finality that follows a death. You can help your children by acknowledging in advance that such occasions will be difficult. Take the time to talk about the sad feelings that your children might experience. Be prepared: Your children may express their sense of loss again and again. If the family is together for a celebration, pause for a moment to reflect on the good times that you shared with the person who died and on the sadness of your loss.

The Five Questions
Children Most Frequently Ask

1. Why did he or she die?

Do not answer this question by citing the person's age or the gravity of the person's illness. Instead, give a simple answer about the physical cause of death. If it is appropriate, you may wish to show your child a copy of the official death certificate. Do not give answers that are more complicated than is necessary.

2. Will I die, too? Will Mom or Dad die?

When children experience the death of someone close to them, they tend to question their own mortality and that of other close family members, especially their parents. A simple and honest answer is: Everything and everybody that lives will die someday. You might want to add that most people in this country can expect to live until the age of seventy-five. If you've had a recent physical exam, assure your child that you are in good health. If you are overdue for a checkup, schedule one.

3. How does a person get to heaven?

To answer this question, you need to distinguish between what happens to the body and what some people believe happens to the spirit. After a person is buried, someone might say, "Now she's up in heaven." A child might respond to this statement by looking down at the grave, looking up at the sky, and asking, "How did she get up there if we just buried her in the ground?" Part of the answer is, "Her body is buried in the ground, and it will remain buried there forever." How you answer the question "What happens to the spirit or soul?" depends on your personal beliefs. Judaism teaches that the spirit or soul returns to God.

4. Where are his or her legs?

When children are given the opportunity to view a body in a casket before the funeral, they see the body from the waist up because usually only the top half of the casket is opened. Should the child ask to see the person's legs, explain that they are still attached and are located in the lower half of the casket. If a child asks to touch the body in order to find out what a dead person "feels" like, allow him or her to touch the person's shoulder. A child may ask why the skin is cold. Explain that a body turns cold when blood stops flowing through it. Such questions are normal and are to be expected.

5. What happens to a body in the ground?

We know that with time, a body decomposes. Because this concept is difficult to explain, perhaps the simplest response to the above question is that about two thirds of our body is made up of water; the other third consists of our bones. When we die, the water eventually evaporates, leaving only the bones. The speed of this process, which takes an average of ten to twelve years, depends to a large degree on the size of a body, the conditions of the ground in which it is buried, and the kind of casket in which it lies.

Glossary

Chevrah Kadisha: A "holy society" that voluntarily prepares a body for burial according to traditional Jewish practice.

Eulogy: A speech about the life of a person who died that is delivered at a funeral by a rabbi, a family member, or a friend.

El Malei Rachamim ("O God, full of compassion"): A prayer chanted at a funeral by a cantor or recited by a rabbi that asks God to protect the soul of the dead person.

Hearse: A large vehicle designed to transport a body to the cemetery.

Kaddish ("holy"): A prayer in praise of God recited following a death; also known as the *Mourner's Kaddish*. A special graveside *Kaddish* is called *Kaddish Le'itchadeta* or *Kaddish Hagadol*.

Psalm: One of the poems in the Book of Psalms, a biblical work attributed to King David.

Shivah ("seven"): Traditionally, mourners stay home for seven days. A *shivah* candle, which burns for the seven days, is lit when the mourners return from the cemetery.

Shroud: A simple white gown that is used to clothe a body for burial. It signifies that all people are born and die equal before God.

Taharah ("purifying" or "cleaning"): The ritual of washing and dressing a body prior to a funeral. When the members of the *Chevrah Kadisha* perform the *taharah*, they recite prayers thanking God for all of the good the person did in his or her life.

Yahrzeit: ("a year's time"): The lighting of a candle to mark the annual commemoration of the death of a family member.